I Can Write Poems

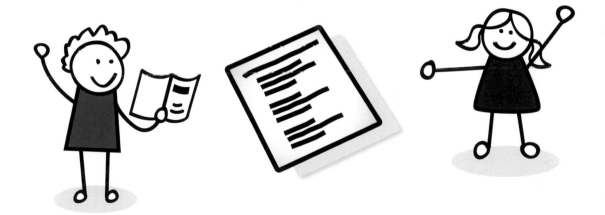

Anita Ganeri

Heinemann
LIBRARY

Chicago, Illinois

www.capstonepub.com
Visit our website to find out
more information about
Heinemann-Raintree books.

To order:
☎ Phone 800-747-4992
💻 Visit www.capstonepub.com
to browse our catalog and order online.

© 2013 Heinemann Library
an imprint of Capstone Global Library, LLC
Chicago, Illinois

Edited by Daniel Nunn, Rebecca Rissman, and Sian Smith
Designed by Victoria Allen
Picture research by Elizabeth Alexander
Original illustrations © Capstone Global Library Ltd 2013
Illustrated by Victoria Allen and Darren Lingard
Production by Victoria Fitzgerald

Originated by Capstone Global Library Ltd
Printed and bound in China by Leo Paper Products Ltd

Hardback ISBN: 978 1 4329 6936 3
Paperback ISBN: 978 1 4329 6943 1

17 16 15
10 9 8 7 6 5 4 3 2

Library of Congress Cataloging-in-Publication Data
Cataloging-in-Publication data is available at the Library
of Congress.

Acknowledgments
We would like to thank the following for permission to reproduce
photographs and artworks: Alamy pp. 5 (© Geraint Lewis),
6 (© Art Directors & TRIP), 7 (© Jon Arnold Images Ltd), 8
(© Lebrecht Music and Arts Photo Library), 9 (© V&A Images),
26 (© Lebrecht Music and Arts Photo Library); Shutterstock
pp. 10 (© Rainer Plendl), 12 (© Elena Schweitzer), 12 (© M. Unal
Ozmen), 12 (© joingate), 13 (© Allaua), 14 (© Tony Campbell),
15 (© Alexander Ryabintsev), 15 (© Inc), 16 (© Pushkin), 16
(© Cienpies Design), 17 (© Meganom), 17 (© HORUSHKIN),
18 (© Jim Agronick), 19 (© Eric Isselée), 20 (© PILart), 21
(© twentyfourworks), 21 (© antart), 21 (© Skocko), 23 (© Amy
Tseng), 24 (© Vasyl Helevachuk), 25 (© Oleksii Sagitov), 27
(© Klara Viskova); Superstock pp.4 (© fStop), 11 (© Fancy
Collection).

Every effort has been made to contact copyright holders of
material reproduced in this book. Any omissions will
be rectified in subsequent printings if notice is given to
the publisher.

Disclaimer
All the Internet addresses (URLs) given in this book were
valid at the time of going to press. However, due to the
dynamic nature of the Internet, some addresses may have
changed, or sites may have changed or ceased to exist
since publication. While the author and publisher regret any
inconvenience this may cause readers, no responsibility for
any such changes can be accepted by either the author or
the publisher.

Contents

Some words are shown in bold, **like this**. You can find out what they mean in the glossary on page 30.

What Is Writing?

You are writing when you put words on paper or a computer screen. Learning to write clearly makes it easier for readers to understand what you mean.

What do you like writing about?

Michael Rosen is a famous poet. A poet writes poems.

There are many different types of writing. This book is about poems. Poems can be **fiction**. This means that they are about made-up things. Some poems can be **nonfiction**. This means that they are about real things.

What Are Poems?

A poem is a piece of writing that is usually written in **lines**. Several lines make up a **verse**. Poems often **rhyme**. They often use words that show feelings or thoughts.

Writing poems can be fun.

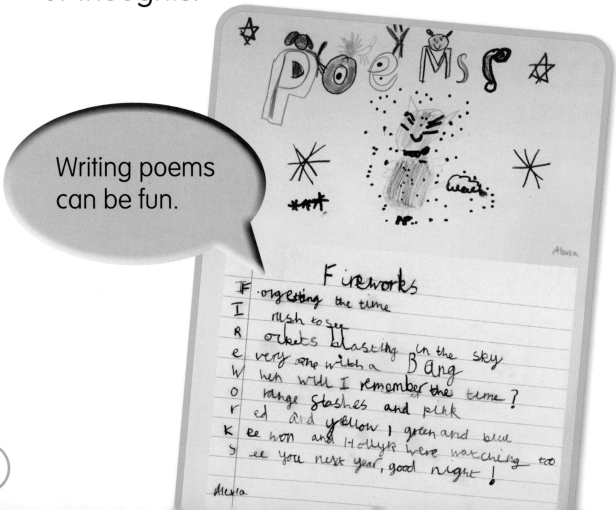

These dancers are acting out a poem.

For many years, poems were not written down. People learned them by heart. Then they told or acted the poems out loud. This still happens in some parts of the world.

Different Poems

There are lots of different types of poems. There are nursery **rhymes**, **riddles**, **limericks**, and **haikus**. Which type of poem do you like reading best?

Edward Lear was an artist and a poet.

It is best to start off writing the sort of poem that you enjoy reading. If you like limericks, read lots of limericks written by other authors, such as Edward Lear.

Getting Ideas

Ideas for poems can come from anywhere! Let your imagination start working or let your feelings tell you what to write. You can also turn memories and dreams into poems.

What are you thinking or feeling?

Jot down any good ideas as soon as you have them.

Keep a notebook and pen with you. Then you can jot down any ideas you have. Scribble down rough notes. You can write them out more clearly later.

Planning a Poem

Thinking up a poem can be hard.
Here are some tips to help you.
Take a word and then write down
anything you know or feel about it.
This is called **mind mapping**.

This is a mind map for the word *summer*.

SUMMER

vacations

beaches

feeling happy

ice cream

sunny weather

Another way is to draw a diagram called a spidergram. Write a key word in a circle. Then write lots of connected words or ideas around the outside.

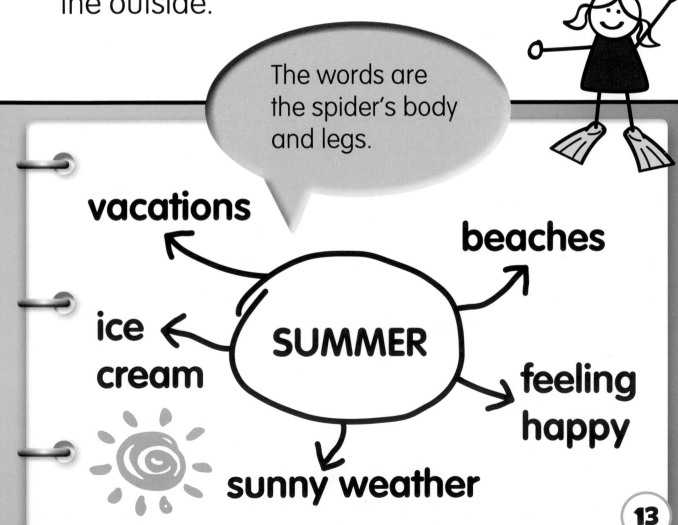

The words are the spider's body and legs.

vacations

beaches

ice cream

SUMMER

feeling happy

sunny weather

Rhyme and Rhythm

Many poems **rhyme**. This means that words at the end of **lines** sound the same. Read the poem below. Can you think of a rhyming word, or words, to fill the gap?

My cat

I am black and furry.
I like to sleep all day!
But if I see a dog go by,
I like to run _____.

You could say "away" or "and play."

Many poems have a **beat** or **rhythm**. This makes them sound more like songs when you read them out loud. It also makes the poems easier to read out loud.

Read this poem and clap out the rhythm.

Rain, rain, go away,
Come again another day.

Words and Sounds

It is important to think about how words sound when you are writing a poem. The sound can help with the **rhyme** and **rhythm**. Here are some words that sound like their meanings.

Can you think of any more?

fizz

hiss

cheep

whisper

bang

Try using lots of words that start with the same letter. This is called **alliteration** (say "al-it-er-ay-shun").

You can use alliteration to create interesting sounds in your poem.

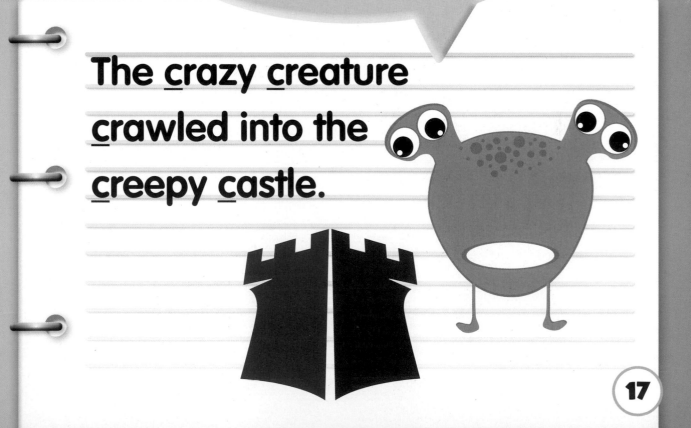

The crawled into the creepy castle.

Acrostic Poems

An acrostic is a simple type of poem. You write the letters of a word down the side of the page. Then, the first letter of each **line** starts a word or phrase.

Sharp teeth

Hungry

Always hungry

Ripping food apart

Killer fish.

This is an acrostic poem for SHARK.

Try writing your own acrostic poem. Choose a short word to start with. It can be something such as your name, an animal, your pet's name, or your favorite food.

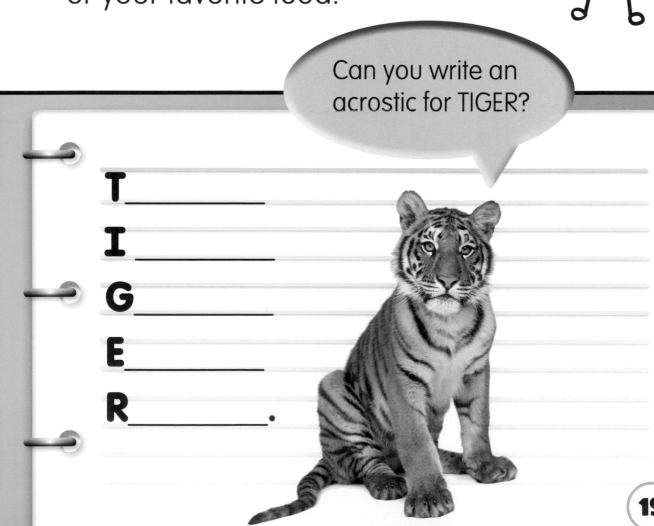

Can you write an acrostic for TIGER?

T_____

I_____

G_____

E_____

R_____.

Shape Poems

You can write your poem in any pattern or shape. Look at the poem below. It is about raindrops. It is written in the shape of a raindrop.

This is called a shape poem.

Drip,
drip, drop,
drop. Rain is
falling. It doesn't
stop. Drip, drip,
drop, drop.

Try writing your own shape poem. Choose a word that gives you a strong shape to work with. You can find some good words in the list below.

Can you think of some other good shape words?

Shape words

heart

star

mountain

ball

tree

Haikus

A **haiku** is a very short poem. It has only three **lines**. The first haikus were written in Japan hundreds of years ago. Haikus follow the strict rules below.

A **syllable** is a separate sound in a word.

Haiku rules

- **has three lines**
- **line 1 has 5 syllables**
- **line 2 has 7 syllables**
- **line 3 has 5 syllables**

Try writing your own haiku. Look closely at something, such as your pet, an object in your bedroom, or the flowers in your backyard. Write down what you see.

<u>Butterfly</u>

Butterfly lands on

flower, flutters, drinks nectar,

flies away again.

A haiku is short enough to be said in one breath.

Free Verse

Some poems do not follow any rules. They do not have to **rhyme**, and you can make the **lines** any length you want. This is called **free verse**.

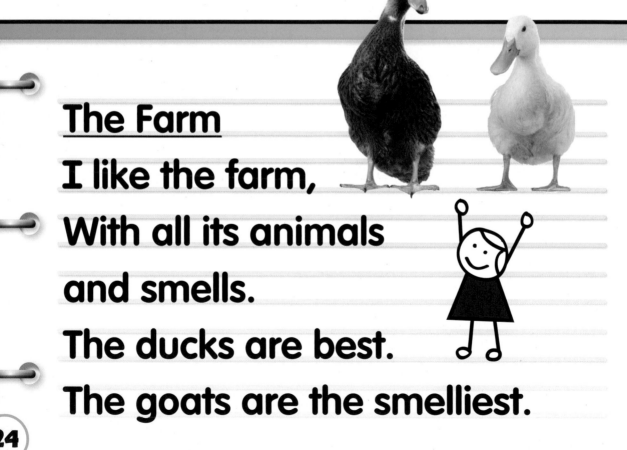

The Farm

I like the farm,

With all its animals

and smells.

The ducks are best.

The goats are the smelliest.

Try writing a few lines of free verse. Choose a subject, such as your vacation or your favorite hobby. Keep reading your poem out loud to get the **rhythm** right.

Think carefully about where to put the line breaks.

Soccer

The whistle blows for kickoff.

I run down the field, fast as the wind.

Dodging two players, I shoot!

The ball flies—it's a GOAL!

Writing a Poem

You have done lots of thinking. Now, it is time to start writing your poem. You can choose a short poem, like a **haiku**, or write a poem that has several **verses**.

The Owl and the Pussycat is a famous poem.

Your poem can tell a story or describe something you have seen. It can be about a special memory or about your feelings. In fact, a poem can be about anything you want.

food

pets

animals

friends

monsters

weather

pirates

vacations

toys

Here are a few things you could write a poem about.

Top Tips for Writing Poems

1. Read lots of different types of poems. The more you read, the better your own writing will become.

2. Read your poem after you have finished it. Check the spelling and make any changes you want. This might take a few times to get right.

3. Read your poem out loud. This will help you check that the **rhythm** is strong and the **rhymes** work well.

4. Use your senses to help you. Choose words that help you write down what you see, hear, feel, taste, and smell.

5. If you cannot think of a rhyming word, write down the end sound and try each letter of the alphabet in front. Pick out the real words that you make.

6. If you cannot think of ideas, try some automatic writing. Write down whatever comes into your head. Then turn it into a poem.

7. Collect all of your poems in a book or on the computer. You don't have to let people read them if you don't want them to.

8. Keep practicing! Writing is just like learning to cook. You need to keep practicing.

Glossary

alliteration using words that start with the same letters or sounds

beat pattern of sounds that is repeated regularly

fiction writing that is about made-up people or things

free verse poem that does not follow any rules

haiku short poem with only three lines. Each line has a set number of syllables.

limerick funny, five-line nonsense poem

line part of a poem that can be a sentence or part of a sentence

mind mapping thinking of everything you can about a subject

nonfiction writing that is about real people or things

rhyme when the ends of two words sound the same

rhythm pattern of sounds

riddle poem that gives clues so that the reader can guess the answer

syllable separate sound in a word

verse group of several lines in a poem

Find Out More

Books

Ganeri, Anita. *Getting to Grips with Grammar* series.
  Chicago: Heinemann Library, 2012.

Magee, Wes. *How to Write Poems* (How to Write).
  Laguna Hills, Calif.: QEB, 2007.

Internet Sites

Facthound offers a safe, fun way to find Internet sites related to this book. All of the sites on Facthound have been researched by our staff.

Here's all you do:

Visit www.facthound.com

Type in this code: 9781432969363

Index